For Jen Edwards, whose idea it was,
and for James, who helped me write it
—K. F.

For my dad and Cindy
—C. K.

Henry Holt and Company, *Publishers since 1866*
Henry Holt® is a registered trademark of Macmillan Publishing Group, LLC
120 Broadway, New York, NY 10271 • mackids.com

Library of Congress Cataloging-in-Publication Data
Names: Farrell, Kate, author. | Kuhwald, Caitlin, illustrator.
Title: V is for voting / Kate Farrell ; Illustrated by Caitlin Kuhwald.
Description: First edition. | New York : Henry Holt Books for Young Readers, [2020] |
Audience: Ages 3–7 | Audience: Grades 2–3 | Summary: "A timely picture book
that acts as an introduction to civics for young readers"—Provided by publisher.
Identifiers: LCCN 2019037072 | ISBN 9781250231253 (hardcover)
Subjects: LCSH: Voting—United States—Juvenile literature. | Civics—United States—
Juvenile literature. | Picture books for Children—United States—Juvenile literature.
Classification: LCC JK1978 .F37 2020 | DDC 323.6/50973—dc23
LC record available at https://lccn.loc.gov/2019037072

Our books may be purchased in bulk for promotional, educational, or business use.
Please contact your local bookseller or the Macmillan Corporate and Premium Sales Department
at (800) 221-7945 ext. 5442 or by email at MacmillanSpecialMarkets@macmillan.com.

First edition, 2020 / Design by Carol Ly
The artist used Adobe Photoshop, digital brushes, and a Wacom screen to create the illustrations for this book.
Printed in Singapore by C.O.S. Printers Pte Ltd, Singapore

1 3 5 7 9 10 8 6 4 2

# V IS FOR VOTING

WRITTEN BY KATE FARRELL

ILLUSTRATED BY CAITLIN KUHWALD

HENRY HOLT AND COMPANY
NEW YORK

**A** is for active participation.

**B** is for building a more equal nation.

C is for citizens' rights and our duty.

**D** is for difference—
our strength and our beauty.

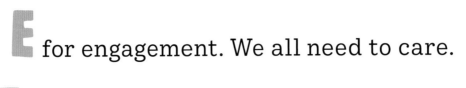

for engagement. We all need to care.

for a free press to find facts and share.

**G** is for govern: to lead and to guide.

# H is for homelands that we've occupied.

is for inching ahead bit by bit.

The march is a long one,
but we cannot quit.

**J** is for judges. They're meant to be fair.
To be neutral, unbiased, objective, they swear.

**K** is for knowing
that you can take part.

**L** is for local, and that's where you start.

# M is for matter—

and every vote does.

**N** is for never forgetting what was.

**O** is for onward.
Keep progress in sight.

**P** is for protest
when we need to fight.

 is for questions. I've got one or three . . .

**R** is for represent.       They work for me!

**S** is for suffrage—the right to a vote.

This fight is ongoing, not history's footnote.

**T** is for talented teachers in schools.

Well-informed citizens don't suffer fools.

**U** is for
unbought,
unbossed,
undeterred.

**V** is for voting to

MAKE YOUR VOICE HEARD!

**W** is working for change,
win or lose.

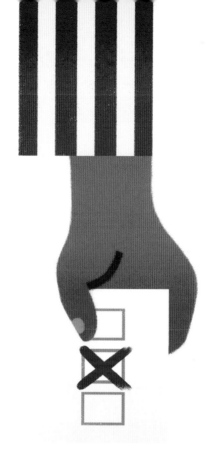

**X** marks the spot on the ballot you choose.

**Y** is for you.
We need everyone's hand.

**Z** is for zeal.

Please bring yours! Take a stand!

In the United States of America, we can influence the direction our government takes with our participation. Voting is one very important part of that. But even if you aren't old enough to vote in an election yet, you can still participate.

## MAKE YOUR VOICE HEARD!

Your city councilperson, your mayor, your state legislators, your governor, your representative and senators in Congress, your president—they all work for you! Write a letter or make a phone call to tell them what is important to you. The addresses and numbers are easy to find online. You can ask your parents or teachers if you need help.

## ORGANIZE A VOTER REGISTRATION DRIVE!

Visit headcount.org or campusvoteproject.org /voter-registration-drive-guides for guidance.

Some of the illustrations in this book depict real people. You might recognize a few of them, but others may not look familiar. Not all of these people held elected office, but all of them are leaders who worked (or are still working!) to build a more equal nation here in the United States, and all are worth learning more about.

## G IS FOR GOVERN: TO LEAD AND TO GUIDE.

*(FROM LEFT TO RIGHT, BEGINNING WITH TOP ROW)* Harriet Tubman, Patsy Takemoto Mink, Sitting Bull, Abraham Lincoln, Jeannette Rankin, Eleanor Roosevelt, Frederick Douglass, Robert F. Kennedy, Mary McLeod Bethune, Franklin Delano Roosevelt

Not everyone has always had the right to vote. This time line highlights just a few of the important voting rights events in United States history.

# A VOTING RIGHTS TIME LINE

**1870**
The Fifteenth Amendment prohibits federal and state governments from denying or limiting the right to vote based on "race, color, or previous condition of servitude."

**1924**
The Indian Citizenship Act grants US citizenship, and thus the right to vote, to Native Americans.

**1787**
The US Constitution is written. It gives states the right to determine who can vote.

**1868**
The Fourteenth Amendment to the Constitution grants citizenship and equal protection of the law to anyone born or naturalized in the United States.

**1920**
The Nineteenth Amendment guarantees women's right to vote.

**1961**
The Twenty-Third Amendment grants citizens who live in the District of Columbia the right to vote in presidential elections.

## N IS FOR NEVER FORGETTING WHAT WAS.

(FROM LEFT TO RIGHT, BEGINNING WITH TOP ROW) Thurgood Marshall, Kathleen Hanna, Ruby Bridges, Harvey Milk, W. E. B. Du Bois, Gloria Steinem, Russell Means, Cesar Chavez, Pauli Murray, Malcolm X

## S IS FOR SUFFRAGE—THE RIGHT TO A VOTE. THIS FIGHT IS ONGOING, NOT HISTORY'S FOOTNOTE.

(FROM LEFT TO RIGHT, BEGINNING WITH TOP ROW) Mary Church Terrell, Ida B. Wells, Virginia Brooks, Fannie Lou Hamer, O. J. Semans, Alicia Garza

## T IS FOR TALENTED TEACHERS IN SCHOOLS.

(FROM LEFT TO RIGHT) Sojourner Truth, the Reverend Dr. Martin Luther King Jr., Angela Davis

## U IS FOR UNBOUGHT, UNBOSSED, UNDETERRED.

Shirley Chisholm was the first black woman elected to Congress, in 1968, and the first black woman to seek a major party's nomination for president, in 1972. Her campaign slogan was "Unbought and Unbossed." Shirley Chisholm's extraordinary legacy has inspired many women to run for office.

---

**1965**
The Voting Rights Act is passed. It outlaws discriminatory voting rules, which many states were using to deny the vote to African Americans, immigrants, and the poor.

**1974**
The US Supreme Court rules that the Fourteenth Amendment allows states to deny convicted felons the right to vote.

**2013**
The Supreme Court strikes down a section of the Voting Rights Act as unconstitutional, allowing states with a history of discrimination to pass new voting laws without federal approval.

**1971**
The Twenty-Sixth Amendment grants eighteen-year-old citizens the right to vote.

**1993**
The National Voter Registration Act is passed, making it easier to register to vote.